Anima Christi is to be prayed da

M000028055

Soul of Christ, sa...
Body of Christ, save me.
Blood of Christ, inebriate me.
Water from the side of Christ, wash me.
Passion of Christ, strengthen me.
O good Jesus, hear me.
Within your wounds, hide me.
Do not permit me to be parted from you.
From the evil foe protect me.
At the hour of my death, call me.
And bid me come to you, to praise you with all your saints
for ever and ever.
Amen.

DAYbreaks

Imprimi Potest: Stephen T. Rehrauer, CSsR, Provincial,
Denver Province, the Redemptorists

Published by Liguori Publications, Liguori, Missouri 63057.
To order, call 800-325-9521, or visit Liguori.org.

ISBN: 978-0-7648-2836-2
Copyright © 2021 Liguori Publications

Liguori Publications, a nonprofit corporation, is an apostolate of the Redemptorists.
To learn more about the Redemptorists, visit Redemptorists.com.

Printed in the United States of America • First Edition
21 22 23 24 25 / 5 4 3 2 1

PAGE 4 ILLUSTRATION ADAPTED FROM *A CATHOLIC GUIDE TO ASHES,* COPYRIGHT ©BILL DONAGHY. USED WITH PERMISSION.

Ash Wednesday

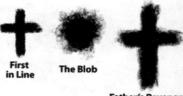

...We implore you on behalf of Christ, be reconciled to God.
For our sake he made him to be sin who did not know sin, so that we might
become the righteousness of God in him.

2 CORINTHIANS 5:20–21

Signed, Sealed, Delivered

Bill Donaghy's *Catholic Guide to Ashes* comically identifies the different shapes and sizes of the dark smudge we receive on our foreheads at the beginning of Lent. Included are a neatly formed ashen cross as "First in Line," an amorphous "Blob," and an oversized, heavily stroked cross as "Father's Revenge."

First in Line **The Blob**

Father's Revenge

While ministering in New Orleans, on Ash Wednesday I saw foreheads bearing what may be mistaken for a flattened palmetto bug. I wouldn't attribute this splotch to "Father's Revenge" but to the aftermath of "Father's Revelry" on Mardi Gras the night before! (I speak indulgently from experience.)

Lent is the penitential season to rejoice within limits. We recognize our short lifespans and limitations, but we rejoice assuredly that the dust to which we shall one day return is glorified in Christ without limit! "The cross, with which the ashes are traced upon us, is the sign of Christ's victory over death"(*Ash Wednesday: Spiritual Medicine* by Thomas Merton).

Thus, ashes are both a sign of mortality and purification in Christ. Before the charred remains of last year's palmetto leaves take fuzzy form on our foreheads, the holy chrism oil first marked the spot at our baptism! "...The person baptized is configured to Christ. Baptism seals the Christian with the indelible spiritual mark...of his belonging to Christ" (*CCC* 1272). Moreover, "The faithful Christian who has 'kept this seal' until the end, remaining faithful to the demands of his Baptism, will be able to depart this life 'marked with the sign of faith'...in expectation of the blessed vision of God...and in the hope of the resurrection" (*CCC* 1274).

If the cross is a bit disfigured on our foreheads on Ash Wednesday, let its distortion represent a desire to reconfigure ourselves to Christ in Lent.

Now's the time to give alms, do penance, and amend our lives!

Thursday

> *If, however, your heart turns away...you will not have a long life.*
> **DEUTERONOMY 30:17–18**

Ad Multos Annos! (To Many Years!)

When people celebrate one hundred or more years of life, they're often asked the secret to their longevity. Some attribute it to abstaining from alcohol; others insist it's because they drink a glass of Chianti every day with dinner. One centenarian recalled an agreement with his wife when he got married at age twenty. The newlyweds decided, that, after any argument, the loser would go for a long walk to let go of the anger. Consequently, the husband attributed his long life to eighty years of fresh air.

Medical science provides sound advice on how to add years to our life, although it often contradicts its findings from previous studies. For example, red meat, eggs, coffee, and dark chocolate are not as bad as we were once told. Cigarettes and soda are worse than we thought. Alas, after giving up red meat for decades, I'm inclined to agree with the saying, "Abstinence is a wonderful thing, but only in moderation." While the common-sense advice to live a life of "moderation in all things" originated in ancient Rome and Greece, the spirit of moderation is implied in Scripture, especially in St. Paul's words of caution about excess, as when he lists "self-control" as a fruit of the Spirit (Galatians 5:22–23).

Hundreds of medical studies have also shown that being spiritual can help us live longer. Even if these studies were to reverse their findings and say that being spiritual can't extend our lifespan, faith can still add fulfillment to our years of whatever number. Prayer, altruism, and a sense of belonging to a community are a prescription for holistic health.

Rx: Meditate, donate, and congregate regularly (and safely) to improve your health this Lent. If your condition weakens, consult your Divine Physician.

Friday

*...The disciples of John approached him and said, "Why do we and the
Pharisees fast [much], but your disciples do not fast?"*
MATTHEW 9:14

A Means to Something Greater

"You will gain more by receiving scorn peacefully than if you fasted for a
week on bread and water," wrote St. Alphonsus Liguori. "It is good to humble
ourselves; but it is much more worthwhile to accept the humiliations that
come to us from others."

If anyone during Lent wonders why we call it a "fast" when it seems to
go by so slowly, let us recall that the Lenten fast in our Church history generally permitted no food at all until noon, and no food or beverages between
meals. The duration between morning and noon was particularly hard on
working people.

No Lenten practice exists as an end in itself. The practices are intended
as a means to something greater. Penances and fasting should be beneficial
to our own spiritual journey, and they should have an outward and upward
effect. Otherwise, "what good is it if someone says he has faith but does not
have works?" If someone has nothing to wear and no food for the day and
nothing is done to meet their bodily needs, "what good is it" (James 2:14–18)?
This is the fasting the Lord wishes:

> *Releasing those bound unjustly,*
> *...sharing your bread with the hungry,*
> *bringing the afflicted and the homeless into your house;*
> *clothing the naked when you see them,*
> *and not turning your back on your own flesh.*

> ISAIAH 58:6–7

A virtuous person "pursues the good and chooses it in concrete actions"
(*CCC* 1803). Lenten disciplines are opportunities to put faith into action, for
a faith that does nothing in practice is thoroughly lifeless.

Saturday

*[Jesus said,] "I have not come to call the righteous
to repentance but sinners."*
LUKE 5:32

Let Us Firmly Resolve

Recall the ambitious list of resolutions often created with good intentions at the beginning of this year—intentions to start walking, stop smoking, floss more, fuss less, lose weight, gain indulgences...you get the idea. If you're like me, a few commitments in this annual ritual were retired quickly. I assured myself there's always the Lenten season to revisit those commitments; or perhaps next year I'll resolve to resist making New Year's resolutions.

For Lent, a minimum of three personal resolutions are good to keep: *"O my God, I firmly resolve, with the help of thy grace, to confess my sins, do penance, and amend my life."* Why?

Confess my sins. "The confession of evil works is the first beginning of good works," wrote St. Augustine.

Do penance. While absolution takes away sin, it does not remedy all the disorders sin has caused. One must do something more to make amends to regain full spiritual health. This satisfaction is called "penance" (*CCC* 1459).

Amend my life. This challenging third component often tempts us to settle for two out of three. Nevertheless, "conversion is accomplished in daily life by gestures of reconciliation, concern for the poor, the exercise and defense of justice and right, by the admission of faults to one's brethren, fraternal correction, revision of life, examination of conscience, spiritual direction, acceptance of suffering, [and] endurance of persecution..." (*CCC* 1435).

First Sunday of Lent

Jesus said to him, "Get away, Satan!"
MATTHEW 4:10

Hellzapoppin: Satan Speaks

U p next, an exclusive interview. Stay right there! But first, a word from our sponsor.

[Thirty-second commercial from Guns R Us]

Welcome back, viewers. Joining us now, live-streaming from Hades, is Lucifer himself to speak about final damnation!

Q. Welcome to our program. The devil. Satan. Grim Reaper. What do I call you?

A. I was offended when John called me "the father of lies" in his Gospel. I prefer, "the father of alternative truths."

Q. OK, Great Deceiver, tell us about your recent accomplishments.

A. I'm especially proud that fewer people now believe in the Real Presence of Christ in the Eucharist. That line from Flannery O'Connor always cracks me up: "Well, if it's a symbol, to hell with it." *[Sinister laughter]*

Q. I thought you'd say COVID-19 was your biggest recent triumph. Are you satisfied with the way the virus became a pandemic?

A. I admit this calamity was bungled compared to the influenza pandemic a hundred years ago. Not enough death.

Q. So, what concerns you today?

A. The total number of abortions isn't what it used to be.

Q. Will the apocalypse include the cosmic and revolutionary cataclysms described in the Book of Revelation?

A. All that—and more! Like the doomsday prophets, I long for a spectacular, Hollywood-style ending, a climactic Armageddon battle! Good and evil going at it! But the secret to ending with a bang is for people to not see it coming. Then, bada-bing, bada-boom! Hellzapoppin! Widespread wailing and gnashing of teeth!

That's why I've devised a three-pronged plan for Judgment Day to come so unexpectedly, a thief in the night would be easier to detect. My cunning plan calls for Doubt, Denial, Division.

[Chyron reads: "Devil Delights in Undetectable D-Day"]

First, doubt everything. The more conspiracy theories people invent, the better. Figuratively speaking, "An empty mind is the devil's workshop."

Second, deny everything. "Climate change is a hoax." "Abortion isn't murder." Get the idea? Hell is paved with the bald lies of deniers!

Third, divide everyone. Tolerance, middle ground, compromise are all harder to justify when the other side is viewed not as your brother or sister, but as an opponent or adversary. Works like the devil every time—between leaders of countries, between parishioners in churches. Fanatics and extremists are legion! My motto is "Divide and conquer!"

Q. I'm afraid we've run out of time.

A. "Running out of time" is precisely what I'm counting on. *[Image fades to black as voice trails]* Until we meet again!

Q. Viewers are already responding to our three creedal questions at #fireand brimstone:

Do you reject Satan? Ned from Poughkeepsie writes, "I doubt that evil exists."

And all his works? "If we deny the life of the unborn, then saving the planet won't matter," texts Lindsey. Adam writes, "If we don't save the planet, then we deny the life of the born and unborn to exist."

And all his empty promises? Our respondents are equally divided on whether Satan's promises are empty.

Now stay tuned for murder, mayhem, and madness on the evening news. Until next time, so long!

[Jesus said,] "Amen, I say to you, what you did not do for one of these least ones, you did not do for me."

MATTHEW 25:45

Acts of Commission or Omission?

Paul F. Boller, author of *Presidential Anecdotes*, said President William McKinley was uncertain about his choice between two equally qualified men for an important job—until he remembered boarding a crowded streetcar one rainy night. One of the men McKinley was considering for the job had also been aboard, although he did not see McKinley that night. When an elderly woman carrying a basketful of laundry struggled into the car, looking in vain for a seat, the man pretended not to notice her and remained seated. It was McKinley who relinquished his seat to the woman. Years later, citing what he called "this little omission of kindness," McKinley decided against the man on the streetcar for the key position.

What President McKinley did for this elderly woman, he also did for Christ!

Catholics are familiar with sins of commission and omission, but how familiar are we with today's parable about committing or omitting acts of kindness? To omit the latter is to lessen our encounter with Christ and forgo a density of God's presence.

We have a responsibility to share what God has given us with "these least ones." Consider the tradition at Jewish feasts of setting aside an allotted portion of fragments—called the *Peah*—for those who had served them: After Jesus had multiplied the five loaves and two fish to feed the five thousand, he told his disciples to gather the leftover fragments "so that nothing will be wasted." The leftovers, filling twelve wicker baskets, were more than they could eat (John 6:12–13).

Tuesday

[Jesus said,] "This is how you are to pray."
MATTHEW 6:9

A Forked Tongue

Children know thirty to forty offensive words by the time they enter school, suggests data from psychology professors Timothy Jay and Kristin Janschewitz, though no one knows if kids are aware of what the words mean.

Likewise, children may not fully understand all the words they use in prayer. I've heard kids not only say—but pray—the darnedest things: "Our Father, who are in heaven, *hollowed* be thy name." "O my God, I am *hardly* sorry for having offended thee."

As children, St. Paul writes, we tend to speak, think, and reason like a child; but we give up childish ways when we become adults (1 Corinthians 13:11). When adults pray "Hallowed be thy name," we are asking God to enable us to give him the reverence that is due; it comes first in the Lord's Prayer before we ask anything for ourselves—a sure sign of respect for God and of our maturity in giving up childish, narcissistic behaviors.

Outgrowing childish ways, however, doesn't mean abandoning petitionary prayer altogether. On the contrary, petitions indicate a total dependence on our heavenly Father, so it is far better for us to approach God in prayer like little children. Even addressing God as Father "belongs to the order of trust and intimacy" (*CCC* 2143).

Saint James writes that, with our tongue, "we bless the Lord and Father, and with it we curse men, who are made in the likeness of God. From the same mouth come blessing and cursing. This need not be so" (James 3:9–10).

When the tongue we use in reverence for God is contradicted by the one used for cursing, consider this prayerful petition:

Heavenly Father, enable my tongue to give you and those made in your likeness the reverence that is due. Amen.

Wednesday

[Jesus said,] "This generation is an evil generation; it seeks a sign, but no sign will be given it, except the sign of Jonah."
LUKE 11:29

Mind Your Manners

Evil isn't a new phenomenon. The Book of Judges, for example, presents a faithless time that may rival what's happening in our world today. The twenty-one chapters are so filled with vandalism and war, murder and assassination, fratricide and suicide, that it makes a grim statement on the worst of humanity.

Observers of our culture offer proof that civilization is rapidly in decline. Consider America's diminishment as a world leader, the seemingly cavalier attitude toward an uninhabitable planet for future generations, and adults engaged in road rage and fatal duels over parking spaces.

Etiquette and manners are reasonable behaviors for civility that society has agreed upon over time. They essentially say: *I dignify you because you are created in God's likeness—even as you answer your mobile phone while I do so!* Manners help adjust the self in a self-centered life.

Sadly, the anonymous social-media environment has created new measurements for what's acceptable. Loud talking on a phone during a show in a theater is unacceptable, and frequent texting during a formal meal in a restaurant or at Mass are frowned upon. But those behaviors pale compared to the loss of civility and respect for others when we see insults, bullying, and threats on social media impair face-to-face dynamics. "There is the dangerous phenomenon of young people becoming 'social hermits' who risk alienating themselves completely from society," Pope Francis warns.

When people use new media to show respect for human dignity, they can transform the world to unite into a global village in unimaginable ways! If we use the new media to hide from the world or to bash people by writing things we might never say aloud, we damage ourselves and others.

Let common decency prevail!

Thursday

[Jesus said,] "If you then, who are wicked, know how to give good gifts to your children, how much more will your heavenly Father give good things to those who ask him."
MATTHEW 7:11

How Do I Love Thee? Let Me Count the Ways

God loves us like mothers and fathers who love their children equally. However, "equally" doesn't mean "undifferentiated." God's love is not a generic, one-size-fits-all kind of love. He loves each of us personally!

God is in the details. From the number of hairs on our head to the delicacies of a spider web or a snowflake, God's level of attention in all things is indicative of his love.

God loves us so much that he allows us to assist in the miraculous creation of new life. But after giving life, God—like all loving parents—can't live it for us.

God's abiding love is so great that he delights in showering us with gifts. Moreover, it pleases our divine gift giver immensely when we, as recipients, show appreciation for his handiwork.

God loves us, not because our actions are always good, but because God is always good. God's love is so merciful that he's willing to overlook any imperfections and weaknesses that make us feel unlovable to him and to ourselves.

Consider writing a passionate love letter to your heavenly Father. Could your prayer be like that of St. Ignatius of Loyola?

All I have and call my own.
You have given all to me.
To you, Lord, I return it.
Everything is yours; do with it what you will.
Give me only your love and your grace,
that is enough for me.

Friday

[Jesus said,] "Leave your gift there at the altar, go first and be reconciled with your brother, and then come and offer your gift."

MATTHEW 5:24

Reconciliation, Not Retribution

The original date palm is highly touted in the Bible for its eye-pleasing, shade-producing, food-bearing, and medicinal properties. It was destroyed by the Crusaders during the Middle Ages. In 2005, Israeli scientists in Jerusalem successfully germinated date seeds from the approximate time of Christ. The seeds, presumably unplanted due to bloodshed, were taken from an excavation at the fortress of Masada, where nearly a thousand Jewish zealots perished by their own hand rather than surrender to an imperial Roman assault in AD 73.

Six weeks after the seeds were planted, the astonished scientists found the earth cracked in a pot and each new leaf looking more normal, as though it had a difficult time getting out of the seed after being dormant for so long.

What if a crusade were led to propagate the Christian concept of loving and forgiving our enemies? Like the dormant seed, we also may have a hard time getting out of the attitude that fosters "an eye for an eye and a tooth for a tooth" mentality. Revenge, after all, is as old as time. However, it isn't retaliation but reconciliation that Jesus highly touts in the Bible for its healing attributes (see Matthew 5:28–41).

Jesus teaches, "Love your enemies and pray for those who persecute you" (Matthew 5:44). What would be the reaction if every Christian church in this country appropriately prayed for the safety of our troops, followed by a genuine petition of concern for the welfare of the people we call our adversaries? Moreover, visualize how vacant the pews and sanctuaries would be if every church applied Christ's law of going first to be reconciled and only then offering our gift at the altar (See Matthew 5:23–24).

How can you cultivate the seeds of reconciliation sowed by Christ?

Saturday

[Jesus said,] "So be perfect, just as your heavenly Father is perfect."
MATTHEW 5:48

Notes to Self

Next to luggage with rollers, note paper with adhesive may be one of the greatest modern inventions. These repositionable notes come in assorted shapes and sizes, and their stickiness doesn't leave a residue.

Lent is an opportune time to take a "notes-to-self" inventory to reposition certain attitudes and behaviors, adhere firmly to resolutions, and leave painful residue from the past behind. Which of these resolutions will stick for you?

Resolve to: make time for more peace and quiet this Lent. Otherwise your clamorous world drowns out the voice of the One who says, "Be still and know that I am God!" (Psalm 46:11).

I'm uncomfortable with silence, because I so seldom experience it. My world emits more noise pollution than a motorcycle rally! The neighbor's lawn service uses two leaf blowers—at 7 AM—every Saturday! A local teenager modified the exhaust system on his vehicle to make it sound cooler. Attempts to enjoy a quiet moment while sipping overpriced coffee at my favorite beanery's outdoor space are often disrupted by blaring sounds from its drive-through.

Resolve to: maintain a better balance between work and leisure, between the agony and ecstasy of life. To reawaken your senses.

I will savor more of what life offers and embrace spontaneity this Lent. Like a classic martini, my routine will be shaken, not just stirred. Over the years, my senses have been dulled by monotonous toil and routine. I've grown accustomed to the tastes of bland coffee and powdered eggs. My life has become as predictable as a nondescript wine sold in a box!

Resolve to: By the grace of God, hold tight to compassion.

"Be perfect, just as your heavenly Father is perfect" (Matthew 5:48) seems unattainable. However, scholars assert that Jesus may have said "compassionate" instead of "perfect." If the IRS loses more than two million tax returns and related documents annually and hospitals give newborns to the wrong parents daily, I'm entitled to a few errors!

Second Sunday of Lent

And he was transfigured before them, and his face shone like the sun,
and his clothes became dazzling white.
MATTHEW 17:2

Transfigured in Christ

Catholic author Flannery O'Connor and her spiritual director were sitting on the porch at her farm in Andalusia in Georgia when one of her prized peacocks appeared before them. Even though it had lost its leg in a mowing accident, the one-legged bird suddenly manifested its radiant peacock display. Flannery whispered to the priest that in medieval times, the peacock was a symbol of the transfiguration of Christ. The priest agreed, but also noted that the preening, flamboyant birds could just as easily symbolize the sin of pride.

On a separate occasion, after one of Flannery's exotic peacocks had unfurled its spectacular tail, an unimpressed repairman remarked, "Never saw such long ugly legs….I bet that rascal could outrun a bus."

On the first Sunday of Lent we recall how Satan appeared before Christ in the desert and radiantly displayed "all the kingdoms of the world in a single instant" (Luke 4:5). Satan, that rascal, proudly clucked that he had the authority to give this power to whomever he chose, but Christ wasn't impressed. Satan's final effort to tempt Jesus in the desert transported them to the pinnacle of the temple in Jerusalem, which anticipated Holy Week and the spectacular defeat of Satan by the cross (Hebrews 2:14–15).

Likewise, the mystery of the transfiguration is understood in the context of the Lord's passion—his "going up" to Jerusalem to die and rise again is why we Christians can be as proud as a peacock on Easter.

Monday

[Jesus said,] "Be compassionate, as your Father is compassionate."
LUKE 6:36

In the Hands of an Inviting God

The Puritans—the English Calvinists who colonized Massachusetts in the 1600s—adhered strongly to their belief in eternal damnation, innate sin, and the power of the devil. H. L. Mencken mused that Puritanism was "the haunting fear that someone, somewhere, may be happy." Likewise, American Baptists were known to even "out-Calvin Calvin."

In his 1741 sermon "Sinners in the Hands of an Angry God," Jonathan Edwards preached that it was solely God's decision to allow sinners more time to repent before imposing a wrathful judgment: "There is nothing that keeps wicked men at any one moment out of hell, but the mere pleasure of God."

Catholics adhere strongly to our belief in the possibility of eternal damnation, innate sin, and diabolical power, but we also believe in the grace of baptism to remove original sin and the extraordinary power of conversion to prevent everlasting damnation. Consequently, God is more inviting than intimidating. Meister Eckhart said that compassion is another name for God.

The Lord God is "gracious and merciful, slow to anger and abounding in love and fidelity."

EXODUS 34:6

Tuesday

[Jesus said,] "All their works are performed to be seen."
MATTHEW 23:5

Genuine Self-Denials

A letter writer to the editor of *Time* magazine lamented that a "boring" white background on the cover of three successive issues made the magazine "look terrible" on her coffee table. Judging a weekly news magazine by its cover for décor may be likened to the scriptural Pharisees whose works were performed to be on display.

Our Lenten practices and sacrifices shouldn't attract an undue amount of attention. When deeds of mercy are performed in secret, "your Father who sees what is hidden will repay you" (Matthew 6:18). Moreover, such sacrifices should be genuine.

If Brussels sprouts isn't a favorite food item, then is giving it up for Lent a true sacrifice or a disingenuous convenience? Is abstaining from meat really a sacrifice for many people, when it's merely replaced by a sumptuous seafood feast? Is giving up a favorite specialty coffee drink for forty days of any great value outside of yourself? In this case, it may be advisable not to deny yourself the enjoyment, but to include an additional resolve to calculate the accumulated cost of these beverages and donate that amount to those in real need.

Flannery O'Connor once ordered a vegetable plate at a restaurant on a Friday in Lent. The waiter confirmed her suspicions that the vegetables were cooked in ham stock. Flannery later told a priest, "I know I ain't going to hell over a plate of butterbeans, but I don't know if I have to run to confession before I go to Communion."

Self-denials during Lent, including fasting and abstinence from meat, are voluntary, not obligatory. Just as our Lord's acts of self-denial and mortification were freely chosen, Catholics may fast before Communion *beyond* the duration and degree currently prescribed.

One authentic, attainable resolution made to an all-knowing God is more desirable than duplicity or guilt.

Wednesday

Jesus...said, "You know that the rulers of the Gentiles lord it over them, and the great ones make their authority over them felt. But it shall not be so among you....Whoever wishes to be great among you shall be your servant."
MATTHEW 20:25–26

On Eagles' Wings

Jesus' teachings differ from those of the scribes. To him character mattered. His authority and integrity were clear from his authentic relationship with God. Moreover, Jesus said to his apostles, "whoever wishes to be great among you shall be your servant" (Matthew 20:25–26).

Thus, in Christ's counterintuitive revolution, the greater the service, the greater the authority! As Christ's disciples, we act with true authority through our relationship to God, which defines our character and which is demonstrated through service. These elements generate a level of dignity for the Christian that comes with positions of authority.

In his book *How to Become a Great Boss* (Hyperion, 2002), Jeffrey J. Fox notes that bullies, tyrants, and autocrats are actually weak, and "their authority is a function of job position, not personal character."

Fox says the eagle is a metaphor for dignity. Those who exemplify authority are like eagles that do not go into the hole for a rat—as do snakes, ferrets, and weasels—because they have too much class to lower themselves to that level of "shouting matches, nasty memo wars, or backbiting."

Today, authority figures with the dignity of an eagle in government, churches, and the corporate world are an endangered species. Some possess an autocratic, imperious style of leadership to mask personal inadequacies and insecurities. Others undermine their own authority, character, and integrity to engage in backbiting and bullying. Others compromise the element of service that's essential in all walks of life.

More troubling is the widespread tolerance of unseemly, shameful behavior and the base form of entertainment that it seems to provide.

Why ask our leaders to soar like eagles if we're content with them—and us—acting like weasels?

Thursday

...My child, remember that you received what was good during your lifetime while Lazarus likewise received what was bad; but now he is comforted here, whereas you are tormented.

LUKE 16:25

Dogged by Obligation

Did you know the three-second memory span for goldfish is a myth?

As a youngster, I invested in a tank of bug-eyed goldfish after the loss of my faithful one-eyed Pekinese companion. That's when "the boy and his inseparable dog" tried to become "the boy at one with his goldfish."

Did I already mention that goldfish have a memory span of more than three seconds? What I found out after close contact with my furry family member is that those who lie down with dogs arise with fleas. Another discovery: my pet savored whatever I disliked on my plate—and I had quite the discriminating palate as a kid.

Jesus told the Syrophoenician woman, "Let the children be fed first. For it is not right to take the food of the children and throw it to the dogs." Just as children are fed before pets, the children of Israel were entitled to the gospel first. In humility, the woman answered: "Lord, even the dogs under the table eat the children's scraps" (Mark 7:27–28).

"Dogs" was often a derogatory term in the Scriptures. The Pharisees would have viewed the beggar as unclean in the parable of Lazarus and the Rich Man because he was outside the gate with dogs (Luke 16:19–31). It was also easier for them to dehumanize beggars when they were placed on a par with dogs. But in this parable, the humans, superior to all creatures, are remiss, for it's the four-legged ones that tend to the beggar's ulcerated sores, despite the two-legged creatures' responsibility to do so.

Is our short attention span easily distracted from our obligation to assist the overworked and mistreated, the underfed and hungry, the lost and forgotten?

Friday

> *[Jesus said,] "The stone that the builders rejected
> has become the cornerstone."*
> **MATTHEW 21:42**

A Virtuous Blueprint

In 1916, architect John Lloyd Wright invented Lincoln Logs. These sturdy, delightful toy sets used to erect model log cabins were especially popular in the 1920s and again in the 1950s and sixties. As I recall the distinctive scent that wafted from the cylindrical storage tin containing the interlocking, stained-wood logs and green slats, I'm reminded of a quote by Wright's father, American architect Frank Lloyd Wright. He said, "The physician can bury his mistakes, but the architect can only advise his clients to plant vines."

While vines may also cover our monumental tombstones, they cannot hide our interior imperfections and vices from the Architect of Life when we are raised up. Lent is an ideal time to inspect our foundation and build upon something we can use for discipleship: Character!

Bishop Fulton Sheen wrote, "Character-building does not consist in the elimination of vice, but in the cultivation of virtue."

Character formation is our greatest construction project in life. Fr. Bernard Haring, CSsR, wrote that our character hinges on the attention we give our individual virtues, but it's never simply one person's private task "but a striving together with and for one another."

Saint Paul calls on us to design and construct our spiritual building "upon the foundation of the apostles and prophets, with Christ Jesus himself as the capstone. Through him the whole structure is held together and grows into a temple sacred to the Lord" (Ephesians 2:20–22).

Virtues, then, are the "Lincoln Logs" that interlock us to Christ. They fit together and take shape when they're constructed on a foundation of solid character. "The goal of a virtuous life is to become like God," wrote St. Gregory of Nyssa.

This Lent, let's build something together!

Saturday

Let us eat "and celebrate with a feast, because this son of mine was dead, and has come to life again."
LUKE 15:23–24

Enter into the Feast

My mother was a consummate cook who frequently preferred preparing food to eating it. To a cousin she once confided that she'd sometimes dance while alone in the kitchen cooking a meal. I relish the endearing image of my mother dancing from sheer delight at creating a meal for the enjoyment of those who would gather to feast on it.

For Jesus, a meal was a way to be with God, which is why he instituted the Eucharist with the command, "Eat and drink in memory of me."

"Our way of thinking is attuned to the Eucharist, and the Eucharist in turn confirms our way of thinking" (*CCC* 1327). In other words, everything people see in us as Catholics we owe to the Mass. In prayerful gratitude, we prepare the Lord's table and ask God to bless our everyday staples of bread and wine and make them holy so we ourselves can become holy. We hunger and thirst for holiness so we can become bread and wine shared to a wounded world; in turn, the wounded help us love God better because of them.

Nevertheless, we hear much these days about people who no longer go to Mass. They're like the older brother in the parable of the Prodigal Son who refuses to enter his father's house. But when we step into our Father's house, do we truly enter into the feast and the dance? If not, are we that different from the prodigal's brother?

"Let them praise his name in dance /
...for the LORD takes delight in his people."

PSALM 149:3A, 4A

Think of the impact on our world if Catholics better appreciated what transpires at the eucharistic banquet. Picture the presider who barely keeps from dancing while preparing the gifts at the altar! Imagine those in the Communion line with a lively pep in their step! Savor the image of our Lord who dances with sheer delight at instituting a meal for the life of those who gather to feast on it.

Third Sunday of Lent

Jesus said [to the Samaritan woman], "Give me a drink."
JOHN 4:7

Foreign Encounters

"Y'all mind sharing a table with these folks?" asked the attendant as we wandered into a dueling piano bar in the French Quarter. Our group was one or two years past the legal drinking age; they were elderly couples, one or two drinks past the legal alcohol limit. The couples were from California visiting New Orleans for an Elks Convention. My Cajun friends and I had limited experience with elks—or their conventions—but thirst knew no boundaries, and lasting friendships with these strangers was formed.

In John's Gospel, two strangers meet at a well on the outskirts of town. Their peoples—the Jews and the Samaritans—had been estranged from each other for generations. Thirst, however, knows no boundaries.

"The woman is taken aback that a Jew, no matter how thirsty, would ...ask a Samaritan for a drink," writes Denis McBride, CSsR. Yet, she "has a thirst for meeting Mr. Right" that hadn't been satisfied after five husbands and the man she's living with. Then the buckets are turned, when Jesus tells her he is the Christ, and "at long last she has met the right man."

Also in this vein about strangers, Jesus tells of a man who was robbed (Luke 10:25–37). Because of their hatred toward Samaritans, listeners would have expected the Samaritan in the parable to be a villain. However, the man who was robbed met the right man in the good Samaritan.

Jesus' surprise ending was intended for those who needed convincing that all people have redeeming qualities—even strangers they least expect.

Moreover, the priest and the Levite in the story were presumably moved with pity for the wounded man, but they did nothing. Compassion leads to action!

When a teacher asked a little girl in catechism class why she thought the priest in the Good Samaritan story passed by on the other side, she replied, "Because the man lying by the road had already been robbed!"

Go and wash…and your flesh will heal, and you will be clean.
2 KINGS 5:10

Inherent Dignity

"The wheels of justice move slowly," forewarned my jury duty summons letter, but the month-long experience at criminal court felt more like the tires had blowouts! So, while serving time with my aggravated battery of potential jurors, I appropriately read Neil White's memoir *In the Sanctuary of Outcasts* (William Morrow Paperbacks, 2010) about his eighteen-month sentence for bank fraud in a federal prison that was also home to the last people in the continental United States affected by leprosy.

"Prisoners and leprosy patients," he wrote, "might have been considered outcasts by most of the world, but we were stuck here together." The author initially feared touching them, but he realized that they wouldn't have wanted him to handle their finances either. Ultimately, in a sanctuary for outcasts, "surrounded by men and women who could not hide their disfigurement," the author faced his own. It set him on the path to redemption.

The incarcerated and those condemned to die are often considered "leprous" outcasts of society. If we believe they're less deserving of human dignity, circumstantial evidence in the *Catechism* points to the contrary. The Church maintains that all human life has an inherent dignity that reflects God's creative power and is therefore worthy of reverence and respect (*CCC* 2319).

Our faith gives witness to the fact that the Son of Man willingly endured condemnation to death, suffering, and disfigurement, when he set out on a path to Calvary and fulfilled God's plan of plentiful redemption. Jesus did not come to release us from human suffering, but to reveal that something good can potentially come from it. Kind of like…jury duty!

Of the seven corporal works of mercy, how challenging is "visiting the imprisoned" (Matthew 25:36) for you?

Tuesday

[Jesus said,] "That is why the kingdom of heaven may be likened to...."
MATTHEW 18:23

What's Your Story?

Parables are short, relatable stories with simple images or comparisons to convey a moral or religious lesson. They form approximately one-third of Jesus' recorded teachings. More than merely nice stories, parables reveal mysteries to believers and conceal mysteries from unbelievers.

After the Pharisees rejected Jesus (Matthew 12:14), he immediately changed his straightforward teaching to parables. Jesus said nothing to the crowds without parables to fulfill what was spoken by the prophet, "I will open my mouth in parables, I will utter what has been hidden since the foundation of the world" (see Matthew 13). Thus, parables confront the hearer or reader with a radical choice to enter the kingdom of God. "One must enter the kingdom, that is, become a disciple of Christ, in order to 'know the secrets of the kingdom of heaven.' For those who stay 'outside,' everything remains enigmatic" (*CCC* 546).

The masterful stories of Jesus put us in touch with the mystery of God and ourselves. For example, the three parables of mercy—the lost sheep, lost coin, and lost son—known as "the gospel within the Gospel" in chapter 15 of Luke reveal as much about God as about us. As John Shea writes in *Stories of God* (Liguori Publications, 2007): "God not only loves to hear our stories, God loves to tell stories. And, quite simply, we are the story God tells." In the telling, we ourselves are told.

The timeless, universal stories of Jesus speak to us at different stages of life and provide multiple levels of meaning to the openhearted.

[Jesus said,] "Whoever breaks one of the least of these commandments...
will be called least in the kingdom of heaven."
MATTHEW 5:19

Sins Against Humanity

When we confess our sins and shortcomings in the sacrament of penance, they may seem insignificant compared to the issues facing our world today. For example, confessing "I gossiped five times in the last two weeks" isn't necessarily a trivial matter in the context of Jesus' warning about breaking the least significant commands, but an examination of conscience should also include "sins against humanity" on a grander scale. What have we done or not done about combatting world hunger, racism, homelessness, and so forth?

Before celebrating the sacrament of penance, ask: *If much of humanity is without life's basic necessities, did I keep the Lord's commands?* Sins beyond a personal level belong in the confessional because Yahweh in Scripture is revealed as a liberator of the oppressed, and Christ viewed himself in the same way. Nevertheless, do our seemingly minor good acts have any lasting effect?

Social action agencies and internet searches can assist our awareness of companies that consistently violate the dignity of fair wages, safe working conditions, and child labor laws (see *CCC* 2434). As consumers we can refuse to buy a product or patronize a business that oppresses God's people and his creation. In doing so, our actions are never insignificant, especially when one informed conscience can influence the family, church congregation, school system, and/or corporate investment committees to which we belong!

The whole power of the sacrament of penance restores us to God's grace and joins us with him. While this is the primary purpose and effect, the sacrament "is usually followed by peace and serenity of conscience" (*CCC* 1468).

God, in this Lenten penitential season, please grant me:
The serenity to accept the things I cannot change,
The courage to change the things I can,
And the wisdom to know the difference. Amen.

The common wording of the Serenity Prayer
is attributed to Reinhold Niebuhr (1892–1971)

Thursday

[Jesus said,] "Every kingdom divided against itself will be laid waste and house will fall against house."
LUKE 11:17

On the Side of Jesus

Ideally, Christianity is challenged to supersede partisanship and division, and its practitioners are called to proclaim foremost the gospel according to Jesus Christ.

Realistically, though, how do we resist the tendency to create a pulpit or soapbox for political loyalties? How do we prevent ourselves from being a special interest group of a political party, especially in today's climate where partisanship foments extremism?

Catholics are not apolitical, nor are we all centrist in our ideologies. We have our biases, which distort the gospels, intentionally or not.

In *The Righteous Mind* (Vintage, 2013), social psychologist Jonathan Haidt writes about how people are often divided by political and religious views. People see confirmation of their grand narrative everywhere, and it's difficult—perhaps impossible—to convince them they're wrong. Try arguing with ideologues by taking a view from outside their matrix. You can't. Essentially then, radical political partisanship allows for little advancement outside extremists' comfort zone or matrix.

A nation or Church divided against itself will fall. In 2017, Pope Francis said when Christians "take sides and form parties, when we adopt rigid and airtight positions, [we] become Christians of the 'right' or the 'left' before being on the side of Jesus." That's because Christ's message doesn't align completely with any political party, despite preaching to the contrary by religious leaders of all political stripes.

A round-the-clock news culture of real and polarizing opinions about the Church and world may, at best, make us better-informed, but what's it doing for our spirituality? Seek greater knowledge and truthful information about current affairs. But stay away from views that promote intolerance of others and compromise our Christian belief in the goodness of humanity.

Friday

[Jesus said,] "You shall love your neighbor as yourself."
MARK 12:21

Possessed by Possessions?

In a San Antonio cemetery rests the widow of a Texas oil tycoon who asked to be buried in a lace nightgown and in her Ferrari, "with the seat slanted comfortably." The Superior Court of Los Angeles found the request unusual though not illegal, so the cost of shipping the car to Texas was deducted from her vast estate. The image of a hearse towing a Ferrari may have given onlookers fleeting hope: *Maybe you really can take it with you!*

The wise, stammering old Benedictine monk in the book *Father Joe: The Man Who Saved My Soul* (Random House Trade Paperbacks, 2005), Tony Hendra writes, "P-p-possessions are extensions of the self, you see....The more possessions, the less likely will be your release from the p-p-prison."

Christians know detachment from possessions is the "get-out-of-jail-free" card that releases us from this imprisonment. But the allure of a winning lottery ticket is that it could release us from "nine-to-five prisons" and provide more possessions to detach ourselves from! Hard-earned riches, and even those won freely, are blessings from God. In theory, no harm comes from owning things or from the pleasure they give.

Christ doesn't condemn the possession of material goods, but he has harsh words for those who use their possessions selfishly without caring about neighbors who lack necessities. He commands us to love God with all our heart, soul, mind, and strength. Implied is the idea that we should love with our pocketbooks, too. Jesus' second commandment is to love others as much as we love ourselves (Mark 12:28–34). When we love one another, God dwells in us and God's love within us is perfected (John 4:12). But love of mammon over God takes us from the reign of God, as demonstrated by the man who "went away sad, for he had many possessions" (Mark 10:22).

God, in the event you aren't laughing on Judgment Day when we attempt to take our money and possessions with us, can we at least redeem our frequent flyer miles to get out of p-p-purgatory?

Saturday

..."O God, be merciful to me a sinner."

LUKE 18:13

Pride: Harmless or Hurtful?

It's natural to take pride in such things as our nation, city, favorite sports team, our children, and our work, but a more insidious pride is our original sin in the Genesis story of the Fall—that is, humanity's original decision to exist in and for ourselves instead of for God and in God's grace. Pride is our greatest obstacle to God's love, for it's an unhealthy love of ourselves. It isn't that God won't forgive the sin of pride; it's a matter of the proud person being too arrogant to ever pray and seek God's forgiveness.

Jesus told a parable about a Pharisee in the temple who prayed, "O God, I thank you that I am not like the rest of humanity—greedy, dishonest, adulterous—or even like this tax collector." But the tax collector didn't even raise his eyes to heaven and humbly prayed, "O God, be merciful to me a sinner" (Luke 18:9–14). Pride, then, is willful arrogance that excludes the need for God's love and damages our love of neighbor through unhealthy comparison. The proud feel unjustifiably great about themselves when they feel superior to others.

By contrast, humble people "recognize the value, competence, and even superiority of others without feeling any less valuable themselves," writes Alejandro Trillo in *Vices & Virtues* (Liguori Publications, 2015). "In their humility, they feel self-assured, confident, and satisfied with themselves." They aren't necessarily burdened with an inferiority complex. In his book *Back to Virtue* (Ignatius Press, 1992), author Peter Kreeft notes that being humble doesn't mean thinking less of yourself; rather it is exhibited by thinking less about yourself.

Humble people are never too proud to beg God for mercy.

Fourth Sunday of Lent

Laetare Sunday

"I know this much: I was blind before; now I can see."
JOHN 9:25

Uncontrollable Joy!

Mark Twain is thought to have once quipped: "A German joke is no laughing matter," which speaks to the untrue notion that Germans aren't funny.

While our faith is meant to be a serious endeavor, it's not defined as "no laughing matter." On the contrary: joyfulness is not a hindrance to holiness, it's an expression of it! *Laetare* means *"to rejoice."*

A spirituality that radiates the joy of Easter is every bit as authentic as one that reflects the severity of Lent, and all the more inviting, too! A Redemptorist classmate of mine liked to say, "None of us are baptized in pickle juice." That also goes for the Easter catechumens and anyone whose faith has soured over time.

According to Karl Rahner, the German Jesuit theologian, "Only the person who has also a gift for affection can have a true sense of humor. A good laugh is a sign of love; it may be said to give us a glimpse of, or a first lesson in, the love that God bears for every one of us." Another theologian, Karl Barth, stated simply: "Laughter is the closest thing to the grace of God."

Imagine what it's like to see for the first time after being blind from birth. How could the blind man in John's Gospel refrain from laughing at the awesome blessing he received when Christ restored his sight? How could his eyes not weep tears of unspeakable joy at his good fortune?

An ancient Greek Orthodox tradition sets aside Easter Monday for jokes and laughter to celebrate Christ's triumph over death. It may be rooted in St. John Chrysostom's vivid image of the risen Christ laughing at the devil, who is at his wit's end. They rejoice!

On Laetare Sunday, delight in our Redeemer who was obedient even to death "so that my joy may be in you and your joy may be complete" (John 15:11).

Monday

I am creating Jerusalem to be a joy
and its people to be a delight;
No longer shall the sound of weeping be heard there,
or the sound of crying.
ISAIAH 65:18B–19B

O Happy Fault!

In *Between Heaven and Mirth* (HarperOne, 2012), Jesuit Fr. James Martin recounts a story by Margaret Silf of two friends who mourned the death of their mutual friend. On her gravesite, they planted what they thought were daffodil bulbs. Imagine their surprise when they returned in the spring to pay their respects and found a crop of onions! They laughed until they cried—and they felt certain their friend was right in there laughing with them.

At the beginning of every liturgical season of Lent—the name is derived from the word *spring*—we solemnly soil our foreheads in remembrance of the Garden of Eden. With ashen faces and grave Lenten disciplines, we till our hardened hearts through purposeful penance, fasting, and almsgiving, and bury the guilt that we won't let die. Then, when we're born anew, our tears of sorrow are transplanted into tears of joy and laughter!

According to Dante's *Divine Comedy*, "In hell there is no hope and no laughter. In purgatory there is no laughter, but there is hope. In heaven, hope is no longer necessary because laughter reigns." Our faith assures us of a God who takes pleasure in his people and delights in being with us!

If "the one enthroned in heaven laughs" (Psalm 2:4), then
that rumbling sound from on high may be God's thunderous,
uncontrollable laughter in our company!

Tuesday

[Jesus said,] "Rise, take up your mat, and walk."
JOHN 5:8

Good Things Come...Just Wait

The hospital nurse announces that you're finally going home today, but shortly before nightfall, you're still waiting for the doctor to sign off on your release. The words *patient* and *patience* are derived from the Latin *patior* ("to suffer"), so we're undoubtedly called "patients" because of the insufferable patience required in hospitals and doctor's offices!

Hermann Hesse wrote, "Before a man needs redemption,...things must go ill for him....He must have experienced sorrow and disappointment, bitterness and despair. The waters must rise up to his neck."

The man who had been sick for thirty-eight years waited patiently for the movement of the healing waters, before Jesus restored him to health (John 5:1–3, 5–16).

To cure the sharp effects of diseases is a great work
to cure the disease itself is a greater;
but to cure the body, the root, the occasion of diseases,
is a work reserved for the Great Physician.

JOHN DONNE

How patient are you at enduring suffering?

*"Can a mother forget her infant,
be without tenderness for the child of her womb?"*
ISAIAH 49:15

Maternal Influences

Recall that Jesus was so moved for a widow in Nain burying her only son, that he raised the young man back to life (Luke 7:11–17). Perhaps Jesus could easily empathize with the grieving widow because of the symbiotic bond he had with his own mother.

Mater Dolorosa, Our Lady of Sorrows, is the title given to the Blessed Virgin Mary for her suffering during the passion and death of her Son, among the Seven Sorrows of Mary. Tradition holds that she was a widow at the time of Jesus' crucifixion.

Visualize Michelangelo's *Pietà*—the only work that bears the Italian sculptor's name—where Jesus is tenderly cradled in his mother's arms after being removed from the cross.

*"As a mother comforts her child,
so I will comfort you."*

ISAIAH 66:13

Expressing the love of a mother for her son, Washington Irving writes, "She will sacrifice every comfort to his convenience; ...and if adversity overtakes him, he will be the dearer to her by misfortune; and if disgrace settles upon his name, she will still love and cherish him; and if all the world beside casts him off, she will be all the world to him" (*The Sketchbook of Geoffrey Crayon*).

Pope Francis said that a world without mothers would be "inhumane, because mothers always know how to give witness—even in the worst of times—to tenderness, dedication, and moral strength."

*How does your mother give witness to your faith?
What's your bond like with her—even if she's deceased?*

Thursday

[Jesus said,] "For If you had believed Moses, you would have believed me, because he wrote about me."

JOHN 5:46

To the Father through His Son

In the Old Testament, to know God's name is to know God. Because God's name was revealed to Moses, the God of the Israelites differed from the pagan gods that kept their names secret. The admonition of God to "not take the name of the Lord, your God, in vain" (Exodus 20:7), ultimately led the Israelites to substitute titles instead of pronouncing God's name at all. "Yahweh" (YHWH) is the most frequent substitute name for God, occurring more than 6,800 times in the Old Testament, more than all other designations combined.

Scholars generally agree that the meaning of "Yahweh" is an archaic form of the verb "to be," as in "I am who I will be." The name, therefore, signifies the creative power of God. Whatever the accurate derivation, "Yahweh" clearly distinguished the God of Israel as the only *living* God.

In the New Testament, Jesus relates to the living God in a personal way as "Abba-Father," because he alone was God's Son. As God's children in Christ, Christians can now relate to God as Father in a more profound way than Israelites of the Old Testament. Thus, the fundamental prayers at Mass are Christ-centered, for in the Eucharist, God sanctifies the world in Christ, and we offer worship of the Father, as we adore God through Christ, his Son.

How is your relationship in prayer to God the Father strengthened through an understanding and appreciation of his Son?

Friday

Jesus cried out, "You know me and also know where I am from. Yet I did not come on my own."

JOHN 7:28

Background Check

Recall what Nathanael said to Philip about Jesus, "Can anything good come out of Nazareth?" (John 1:46). We now know Nathanael's question is a rhetorical one! However, at the time, Nazareth was a small, secluded village in Galilee considered by many to be insignificant.

Galilee—the region where Jesus grew up—was so called because it was practically encircled by non-Jewish nations (the Hebrew word *Galil* means "circle"). Consequently, Galilee had always been exposed to new, foreign influences and it was considered the most forward-looking and least conservative area of Palestine. Ironically, Jesus' radical and unconventional approach to matters will later prove to be too much—not only for some people from his own region, but also for the authorities in Jerusalem.

God isn't impressed with our pedigree or place of origin.
How important are these to you?

Saturday

"Yet I was like a trusting lamb led to slaughter, not knowing that they were hatching plots against me."
JEREMIAH 11:19

Helpless as a Lamb

"Out Like a Lamb" by Catholic author Andre Dubus describes how he and his family agreed to take care of eight sheep for a year. When two sheep died of suspicious causes, the year mercifully ran out before the flock did. Dubus recalled pictures of Jesus cradling a lamb in his arms and how he had called us his flock: "His face was tender and loving, and I grew up with a sense of those feelings, of being a source of them: we were sweet and loving sheep." But after a few weeks of shepherding, he concludes: "I saw that Christ's analogy meant something entirely different. We were stupid helpless brutes, and without constant watching we would foolishly destroy ourselves."

Behold the Lamb of God, behold him who takes away the sins of the world.

Christ the spotless Lamb came to spare humanity from foolish self-destruction. The salvation of the world is in the pastoral care of the Good Shepherd who desires to do for us what we cannot do for ourselves.

Recall an incident where you felt our Good Shepherd protected you from your own foolish behavior.

The LORD is my shepherd;
there is nothing I lack…
He guides me along right paths
for the sake of his name…
I will fear no evil, for you are with me;
your rod and your staff comfort me.

PSALM 23

Fifth Sunday of Lent

[Jesus said,] "I am the resurrection and the life; whoever believes in me, even if he dies, will live."
JOHN 11:25

The Church Glorified

In his book *Afterlife: The Other Side of Dying* (Paulist Press, 1979), Morton Kelsey writes: "The most obvious and striking feature of Jesus' view of life after death and the final state of our existence is that it is a 'kingdom.'" It is social in nature. Since Jesus' repeated message in the Gospels is to love one another unconditionally, heaven appears to be the place where we interact and grow in relationship with other human beings, with the spiritual entities of heaven known as angels, and with our triune God.

Our resurrected bodies are not like that of Lazarus (see John 11), resuscitated only to die once more, but like the resurrected body of Christ—re-created and glorified. Accordingly, our heavenly existence is free from all pain and fear, from all physical and psychological impediments. The work of Elisabeth Kübler-Ross, MD, on near-death experiences shows a consistent report of regret by persons who had to "return" to their body when resuscitated. Virtually all patients reported that they subsequently had no fear of death; on the contrary, they anticipated it.

Some people, though, are terrified by the idea of their demise and are tormented by a grave image of hell. If heaven is relational and interactive, according to Thomas Merton in his book, *Seeds of Contemplation* (New Directions, 1987), "Hell is where no one has anything in common with anybody else except the fact that they all hate one another."

I invariably think about hell in static checkout lines and wonder what your own image of heaven and hell might be. My idea of hell is an interminable wait at a wholesale emporium with a second checkpoint line to exit only yards away from the first checkout line. Nothing fires me up more than this, when there isn't a snowball's chance in hell of getting out of there without losing my religion. "Save us from the fires of hell, especially those in most need of thy mercy!"

Monday

~~~~~

[Jesus said to the woman caught in adultery:] "Neither do I condemn you. Go, and from now on do not sin anymore."

JOHN 8:11

~~~~~

Scarier than Fiction

Bloodthirsty vampires in literature often symbolize selfish exploitation. They use other people to satisfy their own needs. The vampire awakens "and says something like, 'In order to remain undead, I must steal the life force of someone whose fate matters less to me than my own,'" writes Thomas C. Foster in *How to Read Literature Like a Professor* (Perennial, 2014).

A society that denies someone else's right to live or decides that some lives are not of sufficient quality to merit concern and protection is more frightening than any haunting figure in the gothic novels of Bram Stoker or Anne Rice. A culture of death is scarier than fiction because it's contrary to the natural law that human lives are not at our disposal.

The Church calls people to divine precepts even as some of its members fall short. Here, Helen Alvaré—advisor to the United States Conference of Catholic Bishops—makes a crucial point: "While the Church teaches that the act of killing an unborn child is intrinsically bad, it does not teach that the mother who seeks an abortion is also intrinsically bad. There is a difference between condemning an act and judging the guilt of the actor. Only God can judge these women." She adds, "To the woman who has had an abortion, the Church says instead: 'How can we reconcile you? How can we help you to (first) face honestly what happened, repent, and be reconciled to the child, to yourself, to your family, and to God?'"

As a member of Christ's Church, how often do you find yourself hating the sin but still loving the sinner?

Tuesday

The Jews said, "He is not going to kill himself, is he, because he said, 'Where I am going you cannot come'?"
JOHN 8:22

Care for the Caregiver

A counselor told his gloomy new patient, "Lighten up! You need a good laugh. Go to the circus and enjoy a performance by Giggles the Clown." Replied the patient, "I *am* Giggles the Clown."

More surprising than melancholic clowns is the severity of mental depression among the general public. Suicides in this country are at their highest number in decades, and clinical depression is the leading cause of disability in the world.

A growing number of people today—especially women—assume the role of caregiver, not as a profession, but as a responsibility to a family member or friend who's sick, elderly, disabled, or dying.

Nearly half of caregivers assist a parent or parent-in-law; others care for a spouse. Higher-hour caregivers are more likely to experience stress in their duties, which can also lead to secondary traumatic stress (STS) or "compassion fatigue." Symptoms include mental and physical exhaustion, numbness in interacting with others, and difficulty in finding fulfillment in work. Compassion literally means, "to suffer together."

Caregivers—professional or otherwise—on the verge of compassion fatigue must care for themselves as they care for others. Far from selfish, this is prudent. It's hard to give what you don't have. For this reason, St. Mother Teresa of Calcutta required her sisters to take a mandatory year off from their caregiving duties every four to five years. Recall, too, that Jesus was moved with compassion, but he also withdrew to pray and rest with his disciples (see Mark 6:31).

Lighten your load! Go to the circus, an amusement park, the movies, or the chapel to help keep the mental numbness from overtaking you.

Wednesday

[Jesus said,] "If you remain in my word, you will truly be my disciples, and you will know the truth, and the truth will set you free."
JOHN 8:31–32

Lent: A Sobering Season

If you've ever visited New Orleans, you're probably aware that between the Catholic cathedral and the Mississippi River sits Jackson Square. Surrounding the square are many colorful musicians, magicians, fortune tellers, and portrait painters.

The story is told of a Bourbon Street drunkard who sat for his portrait by one of these artists with all the dignity he could muster, despite his unshaven face and disheveled clothing. After the artist had labored longer than usual, he removed the painting from the easel and presented it to his client. "This isn't me," the drunk man slurred as he beheld the smiling, clean-shaven, well-dressed subject in the portrait. The artist, who had looked beneath the man's exterior to see his inner strength and potential, thoughtfully replied, "But it's the man you *could* be."

The Lenten season has a twofold character: "the recalling of Baptism or the preparation for it, and Penance." By these means, Lent "prepares the faithful for the celebration of Easter, while they listen more attentively to God's word and devote more time to prayer....During Lent penance should be not only internal and individual but also external and social" (Constitution on the Sacred Liturgy [*Sacrosanctum Concilium*], 109–110).

During Lent, we look beneath our exterior selves each day to become the saintly person that we could be through social works of mercy.

A truthful self-portrait, at times, may be sobering!

Thursday

[Jesus said,] "Amen, amen, I say to you, whoever keeps
my word will never see death."
JOHN 8:51

Consolations for the Final Graduation

A priest attempting to create a unique marketing edge for his Catholic school was advised, "Claim that one hundred percent of your graduates go to heaven. Then have them prove you wrong!"

Saint Alphonsus Liguori aimed equally high. He believed it was far easier to graduate to heaven if we were prepared for death since our mortality rate remains at a hundred percent. To that end, his book *Preparation for Death* has had several hundred editions since he wrote it in 1758. Many are quick to dismiss the work—even before reading it—as a book of fear. It presents one macabre meditation, which Alphonsus used for effect as an opener, but in fairness, it's only one meditation out of thirty-six.

In Alphonsus' "Joys of Heaven" from *Preparation for Death* (Liguori Publications, 1998), he attempts to describe what heaven will be like:

> *In heaven we will forever enjoy a kind of happiness which, even as eternity progresses, will always be as new as at the first moment we began to enjoy it. We shall be always satisfied, yet always craving. We will be forever hungry, yet always sated with infinite delights, because desires in heaven produce no pain, and pleasure in heaven never becomes boring.*

> *In a word, just as the damned in hell are reservoirs of wrath and fury, so the blessed in heaven are vessels filled with happiness because they have nothing more to desire. In seeing God face to face and embracing God as their Sovereign Good, they become so inebriated with love that they lose themselves in God.*

There's no better time than the season of Lent to call to mind such realities as life and death, heaven and hell.

Friday

[Jesus said,] "I have shown you many good works from my Father. For which of these are you trying to stone me?"
JOHN 10:32

Trials and Litigations

It is said in jest that the reason crime doesn't pay is because it gets you involved with lawyers.

The actions of Jesus involved him with the scribes and Pharisees who were intent on arresting him, even though he committed no crime. On the contrary, Jesus only performed good works from his Father.

Jesus' messianic entry into Jerusalem occurred about a week before his resurrection. Hence, the Sunday before Easter that begins Holy Week is known as "Palm Sunday of the Lord's Passion."

Tradition holds that Jesus celebrated the Last Supper as a Passover meal on Thursday night. However, modern biblical scholarship suggests that the Last Supper could have transpired on Tuesday night. This hypothesis widens the window of time necessary for Jesus' numerous legal trials before Annas and Caiaphas (John 18:13, 19–24), Herod (Luke 23:6–11), Pilate (John 18:28–40), and the Sanhedrin, whose seventy members needed to assemble (Luke 22:66–71).

In today's Gospel, when the authorities again tried to arrest Jesus, he was able to elude their grasp. Ultimately, Judas is the one to lead Sanhedrin officials to arrest Jesus after the Last Supper in the Garden of Gethsemane, where Jesus habitually prayed at night.

Regarding our salvation, philosopher Blaise Pascal noted in *Pensées* that humanity was lost and saved in a garden—referring of course to the gardens of Eden and Gethsemane. Perhaps, then, when Jesus is confused for a gardener emerging from the tomb on Easter (John 20:15), the mistaken identity isn't completely erroneous.

We adore you, O Christ, and we praise you. Because by your holy cross you have redeemed the world.

Saturday

"Is it better for you that one man should die instead of the people?"
JOHN 11:50

A Ransom for Many

After the Fall in the Garden of Eden, everyday human existence seemed hopeless because our relationship with God had been severed. The hope of spending eternity in heaven could no longer be taken for granted. Scripture even portrays God as a forlorn lover who had little delight left in heaven after the separation: "My people have been taken away for nothing" (Isaiah 52:5).

According to St. Thomas Aquinas, God loves us as if we were his god and as if God couldn't be happy without us. A preface at Mass recalls our gratitude to God for Christ's obedience that restored the gifts we had lost by sinning in disobedience: "For you so loved the world that in your mercy you sent us the Redeemer, to live like us in all things but sin, so that you might love in us what you loved in your Son."

Jesus understood his mission as sacrificing his own life as a ransom for many (Matthew 20:28). His fidelity to that mission was even at the cost of death. However, to say that Jesus' death was payment for our sins is not to say that a vengeful God was appeased by the slaughter of his own innocent son. Rather, we are redeemed because of the mutual love between Father and Son, and the love that Christ had for us all when he offered his life.

"It is love 'to the end' that confers on Christ's sacrifice its value as redemption and reparation, as atonement and satisfaction" (*CCC* 616). It is in this sense that Jesus' death was a payment—not one to be exacted—but a unique sacrifice "that completes and surpasses all other sacrifices," when "the Father handed his Son over to sinners in order to reconcile us with himself," and the Son of God freely and lovingly offered his human life to his Father in reparation for our disobedience (*CCC* 614).

Christ "bore our sins in his body on the tree....
By his wounds you have been healed."
1 PETER 2:24

Passion (Palm) Sunday

The whole multitude of his disciples proclaimed,...
"Blessed is the king who comes in the name of the Lord!"
LUKE 19:37–38

Hosanna!

Jesus entered Jerusalem to accomplish his paschal mystery about a week before his resurrection. "The whole multitude of his disciples began to praise God aloud with joy for all the mighty deeds they had seen" (Luke 19:37). They sang, "Hosanna in the highest!"

Rabbi Abraham Heschel wrote, "Music leads to the threshold of repentance, of unbearable realization of our own vanity and frailty and of the terrible relevance of God."

Like an overture to an opera, Jesus' passion is presented at the start of Holy Week. Otherwise, those attending Mass only on Passion Sunday and Easter would hear of Jesus' arrival in Jerusalem and then his resurrection, but no "sacred movement" in between.

Thus, the Sunday before Easter is the threshold of a Holy Week dominated by the passion of our Lord. It's meant to lead us to re-

THE ENTRY INTO JERUSALEM, GIOTTO; THE SCROVEGNI CHAPEL, PADUA

pentance, to the realization of our own human frailty, and to the mighty deeds of God.

Like the lily's trumpet, our throats and hearts are ready to be opened wide to join with all of heaven and earth in singing out the aria of joy at our Messiah's triumph and Easter's annual return.

Monday

They gave a dinner for him there, and Martha served....Mary took a liter of costly perfumed oil made from genuine aromatic nard and anointed the feet of Jesus and dried them with her hair.
JOHN 12:2–3

A Formula for Happiness

On a trip to Tokyo in 1922, Albert Einstein discovered he was without money to tip the bellboy. Sensing the gravity of the *faux pas*, he scribbled a formula for happiness on a piece of paper—not as famous as his $E = mc2$—but isn't it all relative? His note read: "A calm and modest life brings more happiness than the pursuit of success combined with constant restlessness."

Einstein's handwritten note sold for $1.56 million at an auction in Jerusalem. Who says money can't buy you happiness?

Is there a secret formula for happiness? According to Earnie Larsen, "The two deepest desires most people have are: to love and be loved and to believe they are worthwhile and know someone else believes that also. In other words, to be happy we need someone to love, something to do, and something to look forward to."

To love and be loved: In John's Gospel, Jesus visits with friends, Lazarus, Martha, and Mary in Bethany on the evening before his triumphal entry into Jerusalem. They gave Jesus a banquet, at which Martha served and Mary anointed his feet. What happiness our Lord must have felt among his close friends before the events of the week that lay ahead!

Happiness, of course, isn't winning a few bucks in the lottery. It's playing ball with your grandson. Happiness isn't determined by our number of friends on Facebook, but in befriending our Redeemer who tied a towel around his waist, poured water into a basin, and washed his disciples' feet on the night before he died. After performing this service, the master-turned-attendant tipped us with a formula for contentment:

[Jesus said,] "I have given you a model to follow, so that as I have done for you, you should also do."

JOHN 13:15

Tuesday

Jesus said to them, "While you have the light, believe in the light, so that you may become children of the light."

JOHN 12:35–36

Deep Pockets, Silver Linings

"We are dealing with a looted object," observed the president of the Archaeological Institute of America, Jane Waldbaum. "The artifact was poorly handled for years because the people holding it were more concerned with making money than protecting it." The president's statement is ironic, for the artifact in question has to do with a disciple who was more concerned with making money than protecting his Master.

> *Then Judas, his betrayer, seeing that Jesus had been condemned, deeply regretted what he had done. He returned the thirty pieces of silver to the chief priests and elders, saying, "I have sinned in betraying innocent blood."*
>
> MATTHEW 27:3–4

The 2006 rediscovery of the so-called Gospel of Judas, a 1,700-year-old document, involves as much intrigue and mercenary opportunism as are traditionally attributed to the dishonorable disciple himself. Christianity teaches that Judas Iscariot handed Jesus over to be arrested for thirty pieces of silver, and ironically, for decades the fragmentary manuscript known as the Gospel of Judas had changed hands in search of deep pockets with silver linings. Its thirteen leather-bound papyrus pages deteriorated as it traveled among dubious dealers in Egyptian and Swiss antiquities, and even spent years moldering in a safe-deposit box in Hicksville, NY. The Gospel of Judas takes its place alongside the Gospel of Mary Magdalene and other alternative gospels written by extremists deemed too unorthodox for the early Christian community.

What's your reaction when people line their own pockets at the expense of others, at the loss of our cultural-religious heritage, or at the risk of our human survival?

Wednesday

[Jesus said,] "The Son of Man indeed goes, as it is written of him, but woe to that man by whom the Son of Man is betrayed. It would be better for that man if he had never been born."
MATTHEW 26:24

Blood Money

Flinging the money into the temple, [Judas] departed and went off and hanged himself. The chief priests gathered up the money, but said, "It is not lawful to deposit this in the temple treasury, for it is the price of blood." After consultation, they used it to buy the potter's field as a burial place for foreigners. That is why that field even today is called the Field of Blood.
MATTHEW 27:5–8

The Acts of the Apostles records Judas' *coup de grace* differently, indicating that Judas "bought a parcel of land with the wages of his iniquity, and falling headlong, he burst open in the middle, and all his insides spilled out" (Acts 1:18). The author of Acts adds that the inhabitants of Jerusalem named the property Field of Blood after this ghastly occurrence.

However, accounts in both Matthew and Acts agree that Judas suffered an ignominious demise and the money he received for betraying Jesus was used to purchase a plot of land, commonly known as the Field of Blood. For some good to emerge from this tragedy of betrayal and death, the site where potters collected red clay for ceramics became a cemetery for those who could not afford a burial plot.

The term potter's field is still used today to name the burial place for indigent, unknown, or unclaimed people. For example, at the height of the COVID-19 pandemic, plain wood coffins were stacked in mass graves on Hart Island, the potter's field for New York City.

***What can you do to bring about good
when the next tragedy strikes?***

Holy Thursday

For as often as you eat this bread and drink the cup, you proclaim the death of the Lord until he comes.

1 CORINTHIANS 11:26

Eucharistic Miracles

Miracle, from the Latin *mirus,* means "wonderful." It is derived from an Indo-European root meaning "to smile." That reminds me of a sign: "If it's difficult, we do it immediately. If it's impossible, it takes a little longer. Miracles by Appointment Only." Let's consider the miraculous nature of the Eucharist.

"One single Mass gives more honor to God than all the penances of the saints, the labors of the apostles, the sufferings of the martyrs, and even the burning love of the Blessed Mother of God," said St. Alphonsus.

Sunday Mass is the greatest miracle in the world: the celebration of the Eucharist. God speaks through Scripture. The Church offers a sacrifice of thanksgiving. The Holy Spirit transforms the gifts of bread and wine into the Body and Blood of Christ. The faithful share Communion with one another and with God. So nourished, the people of God go forth into the world to preach the gospel and to live by its demands.

REV. PAUL TURNER, *LET US PRAY*
(LITURGICAL PRESS, 2012)

People come to know Catholics by the stories we tell—as St. Paul told the Christians in Corinth:

For I received from the Lord what I also handed on to you, that the Lord Jesus, on the night he was handed over, took bread, and, after he had given thanks, broke it and said, "This is my body that is for you. Do this in remembrance of me." In the same way also the cup, after supper, saying, "This cup is the new covenant in my blood. Do this, as often as you drink it, in remembrance of me."

1 CORINTHIANS 11:23–25

Experience the Eucharist, the great miracle.
No appointment necessary!

Good Friday

There they crucified him, and with him two others, one on either side,
with Jesus in the middle.
JOHN 19:18

Forget Not this Hour

On Good Friday morning, April 14, 1865, Mary Todd Lincoln told her husband, Abraham Lincoln, she had acquired tickets to a show, *Aladdin, or the Wonderful Lamp,* at Grover's Theatre for that night. But she desired instead to see the nation's most popular comic actress, Laura Keene, play at Grover's main competition, Ford's Theatre. That night, the president was shot to death at Ford's.

Legend has a fateful meeting between Jesus and Dismas—the name given to the penitent thief crucified alongside him. Prior to their final hours on Calvary, Jesus and Dismas first met when the Holy Family had taken flight to Egypt. The story goes that Joseph and Mary encountered robbers along the way who wanted to kill them and confiscate their few possessions. Dismas was one of the robbers. He refused to allow the family any harm and said of Jesus, "O most blessed of children, if a time comes for having mercy on me, then remember me, and forget not this hour." Dismas found forgiveness and mercy in his final hours on the cross.

Prayer Before a Crucifix

Look down upon me, good and gentle Jesus
while I humbly kneel before you,
and I pray that you instill in my heart the virtues
of faith, hope, and charity; true repentance for my sins;
and a firm purpose of amendment.
While I contemplate your five wounds, with great love and tender pity,
I call to mind the words which David, your prophet, said of you:
"They have pierced my hands and my feet.
They have numbered all my bones."

Lord Jesus, have mercy on me a sinner.
Holy Mary, Mother of God, pray for us sinners, now and at the hour of our death. Amen.

Holy Saturday (Easter Vigil)

If, then, we have died with Christ, we believe that we shall also live with him.
ROMANS 6:8

Lord of the Dance

When was the last time you danced? I posed that question in an Easter Vigil homily one year. For some the answer was, "During the Roosevelt administration—Franklin's—when jazz and the jitterbug were the cat's pajamas." Although I had asked this question in a health-care facility of priests and brothers in their seventies, eighties, and nineties, the congregation included people who had displayed fancy footwork doing the Twist and the Mashed Potato in the late 1950s; the Monkey, the Jerk, the Funky Chicken in the 1960s; and disco, a fever that ailed me in the 1970s.

I digress to acknowledge that as a teenager, I participated in a charity dance marathon in our school gym. My dance partner and I dazzled the judges with an elaborate pretzel-like arm formation. After performing nonstop interpretations of the Hustle, my two left feet spent the next night at home propped on the sofa while I watched *Starsky & Hutch*.

"Join in our Master's rejoicing....The rich and poor sing and dance together," exclaimed a homilist on Easter in the fourth century. Our Savior's death has liberated us from even the fear of that unselfconscious, spontaneous kind of dance that's propelled by our delight in God's plentiful redemption. In "The General Dance," Thomas Merton wrote, "The Lord plays and diverts Himself in the garden of His creation, and if we could let go of our own obsession with what we think is the meaning of it all, we might be able to hear His call and follow Him in His mysterious, cosmic dance." Picture Father, Son, and Holy Spirit interlocked in a sacred *pas de trois*...then inviting us to join in.

Easter is an ideal time to engage with the Lord of the dance. Put aside inhibitions and reflect on our blessings of family, friends, freedoms, and faith, to name only a few. Forgo bewailing of our fears and failings, too. Then, in a moment of total surprise, we just might jump to our feet from the couch, grab a loved one, pick up a child, or take a guardian angel by the wing and dance for no reason other than the love of God in our heart! Disco ball, optional.

Easter

If then you were raised with Christ...
think of what is above, not of what is on earth.
COLOSSIANS 3:1–2

Overshadowed by Death, Light Has Arisen (Matthew 4:16)

Easter takes place on the first Sunday following the first full moon after the vernal equinox (the first day of spring).

Astronauts who have flown into outer space are the first human beings to leave earth and look back at it, and the one observation they all report is how beautiful and fragile the earth appears.

An astronaut from the Apollo 14 mission describes what it's like to be alone in a spacecraft built for three passing through the quarter of the moon that is totally unlit by earth light or sunlight: "As you pass through this total darkness, it is so incredibly dark you almost...feel it. And the spacecraft drops in temperature, and with condensation on the bulkhead it gets a clammy feeling to it. So here you are feeling this darkness, and then suddenly the sunlight comes in the window with no warning....Around the moon, one instant you're in total darkness, with all of these feelings, and then the next instant it's sunlight, and you just feel good."

The followers of Jesus were experiencing the darkness of despair when suddenly a light emerged from the clammy tomb: "Very early when the sun had risen, on the first day of the week [the women], came to the tomb." [They were told] "He has been raised; he is not here" (Mark 16:2, 6).

Lord Jesus, early in the morning of your resurrection, you made your love known and brought the first light of dawn to those who dwell in darkness. Your death has opened a path for us. Do not enter into judgment with your servants; let your Holy Spirit guide us together into the land of justice. Amen.

Monday

Peter stood up with the Eleven, raised his voice, and proclaimed...
"You who are Jews, indeed all of you staying in Jerusalem....
God has raised this Jesus; of this we are all witnesses."
ACTS 2:14, 32

Amazing Grace

When the Catholic author Flannery O'Connor was hospitalized in Georgia for lupus, a woman in admissions asked her what she did for a living. O'Connor responded that she was a writer. "A what?" "A writer," repeated O'Connor. Whereupon the woman demanded, "How do you spell that?"

In the writings of St. Alphonsus Liguori, he didn't merely refer to himself as a "sinner"; he was a "wretched" one, to be precise. In fact, he said that the more wretched he was, the more entitled he was to rely on Mary's assistance, for God destined her to be the refuge of the most abandoned.

"Taking into account the fact that our sins affect Christ himself, the Church does not hesitate to impute to Christians the gravest responsibility for the torments inflicted upon Jesus, a responsibility with which they have all too often burdened the Jews alone" (*CCC* 598). Saint Francis of Assisi said it bluntly: "It is you who have crucified him and crucify him still, when you delight in your vices and sins" (*Admonitio* 5, 3).

Alphonsus loved Christ all the more because the Redeemer readily endured his sufferings for our wretched sinfulness. "The nails cry, love; the scourge cries, love; the wounds cry, love!" Consequently, Alphonsus made it his life-long mission to enflame souls with a love for Christ through his passion.

Theologian Anselm of Canterbury had a name for what Christ did for us on the cross: "substitutionary atonement." ("How do you spell that?") What matters most, however, is to fall in love with Christ all over again through his passion!

Prayerfully consider how amazing is God's grace
to "save a wretch like me!"

Tuesday

> *Peter [said,] "Repent and be baptized, every one of you, in the name of Jesus Christ for the forgiveness of your sins; and you will receive the gift of the holy Spirit."*
> **ACTS 2:38**

Baptized in the Spirit

"I just want to know what I can do in the air and what I can't" isn't a plea from an exasperated passenger on an overbooked flight. Rather, it's from *Jonathan Livingston Seagull,* Richard Bach's popular book from 1970 about self-perfection. Jonathan the gull pushes himself to soar higher and fly carefree—in other words, with no baggage or ticket-change fees. The secret, he's told, is "to begin by knowing that you have already arrived." And here's another secret that applies to air travel today: If God had intended us to fly, airport security lines would move a lot faster!

The Paraclete—not to be confused with parakeet—is symbolized as a bird. But what is it? In 1880, the Jesuit poet Gerard Manley Hopkins wrote, "A Paraclete is one who comforts, who cheers, who encourages, who persuades, who exhorts, who stirs up, who urges forward."

Years ago, a sensation occurred at a Mass commemorating our Lord's baptism when a charismatic pigeon found its way inside the church and appeared at the right times and places. At the greeting, "the Holy Spirit be with you all," the bird remarkably took its cue and swooped down the main aisle. At the Gospel proclamation, "...and behold, the heavens were opened [for him], and he saw the Spirit of God descending like a dove [and] coming upon him," the bird in the church hovered directly above the altar before landing on it during part of the homily. Skeptics covered their heads and attributed the bird's movements to coincidence, but others took a more spiritual bird's-eye view: They interpreted it as a sign that God the Holy Spirit is present among us by our baptism, stirring us up, cheering us on, and assuring us—to borrow words from Jonathan—we "have already arrived."

Wednesday

Recall the wondrous deeds he has done,
his wonders and words of judgment.
PSALM 105:5

What Makes You Happy?

On Pentecost, the giddy disciples of Jesus were filled with the Holy Spirit and began to speak about the mighty acts of God in various tongues.

They were all astounded and bewildered, and said to one another, "What does this mean?" But others said, scoffing, "They have had too much new wine." Then Peter stood up with the Eleven, raised his voice, and proclaimed to them, "...These people are not drunk, as you suppose, for it is only nine o'clock in the morning."

ACTS 2:12–15

Saint Augustine called *Alleluia* "joy without words." The word itself is so peculiar it sounds like we're either speaking in tongues, babbling like a child, or inebriated like a patron on Bourbon Street. Hallelujah is a transliteration of two Hebrew terms meaning, "Praise the Lord!" It's an attempt to express our inexpressible happiness after a sobering Lenten season. "In the presence of the mystery that we celebrate on Easter, the mystery of our redemption, our usual intelligible vocabulary is inadequate; when faced with the super abundant mercy of God we can only stammer in amazement like children," wrote Balthasar Fischer in *Signs, Words, and Gestures* (Pueblo Publishing, 1981).

Yet, the sheer repetition of Alleluia throughout the Easter season won't instill happiness in the one uttering it, if a personal experience of God's profound love and mercy is lacking. How can our ecstatic hearts keep from singing Alleluia, if to know God is to feel elation? This, of course, begs the question: What makes you happy?

Thursday

The disciples recounted what had happened on the road to Emmaus and how they had come to know Jesus in the breaking of bread.
LUKE 24:35

Are We There Yet?

While even the stay-at-homes are travelers in our Pilgrim Church, spiritual journeys are nothing new in our faith tradition. Pope St. John Paul II wrote that pilgrimages "have always been a significant part of the life of the faithful, assuming different cultural forms in different ages." Pilgrims were a prevalent sight on the roads of Europe from the beginnings of Christianity to the early modern age. The pious walked barefoot for months and years, while some in Chaucer's day joined the first "package tours," but the purpose for spiritual travel remains timeless: "it is an exercise of practical asceticism, of repentance for human weaknesses, of constant vigilance over one's frailty, of interior preparation for a change of heart" *(Incarnationis Mysterium,* 7).

Despite uphill climbs, divergences, and wayward paths, life is a continuous journey toward the Father, who lent his Son to us so we can experience the total depth of God's unconditional love!

At times we are blessed with meeting new people who enrich us. Sadly, they often go their way as we go ours, perhaps leaving us feeling we have a void to fill. So, we may finally start that Big Project that we just knew would make us completely happy. But that doesn't do the trick, either. In *The Collar* by Jonathan Englert, a passage urges us to "measure the road well [and] make the most of occasions" when we gather by the roadside to break bread together and compare directions. A barbecue with neighbors. A family picnic. A walk with a grandchild. After all, in life, our attitude can make the usual extraordinary.

The joy is and must remain in the journey.

Friday

Jesus said to them, "Come, have breakfast." And none of the disciples dared to ask him, "Who are you?" because they realized it was the Lord.
JOHN 21:12

A Ghost with an Appetite

Simon Peter had more questions than answers as he picked his teeth with a fish bone. *How can he come and go like a ghost? How can he be completely changed in appearance, yet we still recognize him?*

The wafting smell of bread and fish seared on a charcoal fire reached Peter and the other disciples as their boat came to the shore of the Sea of Tiberias. Jesus beckoned them to join him for breakfast as he served the blackened fish. The breeze on the sandy shore made the bread multi-grained. The idea of a ghost with an appetite was too hard for Peter to swallow during this third appearance of Jesus to his disciples after being raised from the dead (see John 21:1–14).

It's clear that Jesus did not simply return to his earlier life after the resurrection, and in one sense, neither should we as an Easter people. Jesus is still alive and among us when we recognize him in the breaking of the bread and in the broken lives, hearts, and dreams of others.

In the early Church, liturgical songs and hymns acclaimed God for having exalted and glorified Jesus as Lord after his death (see 1 Thessalonians 4:14 and 1 Timothy 3:16). At Mass, the community acclaims this mystery of faith during the eucharistic prayer, usually in song:

We proclaim your Death, O Lord,
and profess your Resurrection
until you come again.
When we eat this Bread and drink this Cup,
we proclaim your Death, O Lord,
until you come again.
Save us, Savior of the world,
for by your Cross and Resurrection
you have set us free.

Saturday

"What are we to do with these men? Everyone living in Jerusalem knows that a remarkable sign was done through them, and we cannot deny it."
ACTS 4:16

No Fear!

The popular expression, "No Fear" captures the thinking of many young people today. This bold message is emblazoned on T-shirts, baseball caps—even sports equipment.

In the biblical post-resurrection accounts, the disciples' cowering fear gives way to bold confidence! Unlocked and released from the upper room, they become fearless. Now, even death has no sting, "no fear" for them! They're completely transformed in their courageous actions and outlook on life.

Saint Paul wrote, "You should put away the old self of your former way of life...and put on the new self, created in God's way" (Ephesians 4:22–24).

Metaphorically, at the beginning of Lent we shed our merrymaking to put on an extended sackcloth garment, and now our heads have found the opening—like a turtle emerging from its shell—to be clothed in the robe of salvation at Easter! Even our churches that were stripped during Lent, are now adorned with dazzling apparel: banners, altar cloth, and vestments. Why? Because Mary Magdalene and the disciples hurried to the tomb on the first Easter morning to discover the burial cloth that Jesus had shed, and to hear an angel dressed in dazzling white tell them, "He has been raised just as he said" (Matthew 28:6). Alleluia!

Let us go into the world and proclaim this Good News to all creation—fearlessly!

Second Sunday of Easter

"My Lord and my God!"
JOHN 20:28

You Probe Me and You Know Me (Psalm 139)

T he Church of Santa Croce in Rome has amassed a treasure of relics pertaining to the passion of Christ. This collection includes the largest hunk, a five-foot section of the cross that held the "good thief," a portion of the true cross, the largest fragment of the inscription that was put on Jesus' cross, two spikes from his crown of thorns, a nail, and a part of the pillar of scourging.

Also enclosed in a glass reliquary is another coveted item—the celebrated finger of the Apostle Thomas that inspected the wounds of Jesus caused by the nails. (Lest I sound doubtful, how do we know if St. Thomas was left-handed or right-handed?) Nevertheless, perhaps the "Doubting Thomas" should be better known as the "Probing Thomas"—literally and figuratively.

In order for the Apostle Thomas to believe, he had to feel the wounds on the hands of Christ and touch his side to examine the spear wound. While we're all free to doubt and probe our belief in the resurrected Jesus, "Blessed are those who have not seen and have believed."

G. K. Chesterton wrote, "This historical case for the resurrection is that everybody else, except the apostles, had every possible motive to declare what they had done with the body, if anything had been done with it. The apostles might have hidden it in order to announce a sham miracle, but it is very difficult to imagine men being tortured and killed for the truth of a miracle which they knew to be a sham" (*As I Was Saying,* 1936).

The Apostle Thomas' initial skepticism in Christ's resurrection was replaced by his unswerving belief in it when he proclaims, "My Lord and my God!" Ultimately, Thomas is killed for this truth, martyred in the name of Christ.

Throughout the Easter season, there is no better repetitive prayer that is fundamental to our faith than "My Lord and my God!"

"My Lord and my God!"

JOHN 20:28

Jesus Christ is alive and among us!

In these daily reflections, Fr. Byron Miller, CSsR, shows us where we can find Christ in ourselves and others. It's a journey from the revelry of Mardi Gras, to long walks in fresh air, to Calvary and the road to Emmaus.

From Ash Wednesday through the Easter Octave, Fr. Byron—employing a a light and insightful style—provides opportunities for personal reflection, prayer, and meditation while expanding our understanding of repentance, sacrifice, and support of others.

Fr. Byron Miller, CSsR, is president and publisher of Liguori Publications in Liguori, Missouri. Formerly, he was director of the National Shrine of Blessed Francis Seelos and vice postulator of the Seelos canonization cause. Ordained a Redemptorist priest in 1990, Fr. Byron served on the Liguori Publications Board (2006–08) and on the Extraordinary Council of the Denver Province of the Redemptorists (2005–07).

ON THE COVER AND BACK COVER DETAIL: *NOLI ME TANGERE*, GIOTTO; THE SCROVEGNI CHAPEL, PADUA

ISBN 978-0-7648-2836-2

Liguori
PUBLICATIONS
A Redemptorist Ministry

9 780764 828362